Sauce Will
Thicken
^{on} Standing

Hey Jo!
    From Brilliance
Ignition to Nild
Swimming + beyond,
thanks for being you,
ever inspirational +
continuing to ignite
with your fire! Hope
you enjoy these words!
Rachael B.

From Brilliant
Swimming + beyond,
ever inspirational +
continuing to ignite
with your fire! Hope

Sauce Will Thicken ^{on} Standing

Rachael B.

ISBN 978-1-913590-96-3 Paperback
ISBN 978-1-913590-97-0 Ebook

The Unbound Press
www.theunboundpress.com

For Mum [Jeanette Bell, 1952–2007]
& my biggest inspirations,
Lizzie, Lawrence, and Oberon x

Hey unbound one!

Welcome to this magical book brought to you by The Unbound Press. At The Unbound Press we believe that when women write freely from the fullest expression of who they are, it can't help but activate a feeling of deep connection and transformation in others. When we come together, we become more and we're changing the world, one book at a time!

This book has been carefully crafted by both the author and publisher with the intention of inspiring you to move ever more deeply into who you truly are.

We hope that this book helps you to connect with your Unbound Self and that you feel called to pass it on to others who want to live a more fully expressed life.

With much love,
Nicola Humber

Founder of The Unbound Press
www.theunboundpress.com

CONTENTS

Dear Friend,

Thank you for picking up this book and joining me in my world. I hope that the words you find within also add something to yours.

This collection is a journey… It speaks to my journey as a poet, as well as the more general journey of life. Some of these poems I 'released' as free pdf downloads years ago, but most I didn't publish at all before now because… well, if I'm honest, because I didn't think they were 'good enough'. I can't say I was rejected because I never submitted this collection in its entirety until I got in touch with the Unbound Press about another project entirely!

These poems were all birthed between 2001 and 2021 (with just a few exceptions). During lockdown, I finally pulled them all together, requested feedback and then… did nothing. Until now. Having sent an initial draft of this collection as an afterthought, I later realised (as I lightly edited it before sending) that these poems represent an important part of my journey – from my first time stepping onto a spoken word stage in the early 2000s, to this, publishing my first collection. My second collection will be amplifying other women's voices alongside mine and empowering us all; this one is simply putting my own voice out there, finally, and having blind faith that someone will want to read it, and that you may perhaps find aspects of your own journey reflected here.

Initially, I couldn't decide how to separate these poems – do I include them by subject, date written (which in some cases I am not even sure of!), whether they were written for stage or page, or some other way? In the end, working with the Unbound team allowed me to trust my intuition and simply go with what *felt* right instead of what perhaps more traditional publishers might say I 'should' have done. Much like my poetry – which rarely follows any rules that feel restrictive – I want these words to be free, and for you to be free to interpret them according to your experience of them.

Finally, the title poem, *Sauce will thicken on standing,* is included at the end of the meditation section as this poem is indeed a meditation. When cooking, for the sauce to end up just right – although it may look 'wrong' and *feel* like you should be doing something to make it better – it's often best to just leave it alone, and let time work its magic.

With love,

Rachael

ON POETRY

'Why do you write?'

At many points, I've been asked why I write. Aged about seven or maybe eight, I was asked why I was writing down everything that was happening around me. I shrugged and said, 'Because I'm bored.' But it wasn't just that. I was observing life as it happened, making sense of it by translating it into words I could understand.

A little later, friends would ask me why I'd be writing poems when I didn't have to (i.e. it wasn't homework). I couldn't answer then, not really. But writing poetry to me was like doodling, playing sports, or dancing to them. By getting into my head, I could make sense of my jumbled, somewhat hectic thoughts and emotions, and then 'get out of my head'. Turn off my 'washing machine mind', as I now call it.

I especially liked getting into the minds of others and trying to understand why they thought the way they did. This fascination with the different ways humans interpret the world around us led me to study psychology, and later, NLP and coaching, and more recently, neurodiversity and no doubt more related research in future!

This section of poetry charts my many attempts to explain why I write. If I had to answer this question succinctly (which I struggle with!), it would probably be:

'Because it helps me think. I can't not write.'

Why I write

I write because
sometimes I feel like I don't have a choice,
like if I were to stop writing...
Then I might lose my voice.

Sometimes I write just because I like the way certain words sound
together...
I write for ego –
I get to leave behind something that will last forever.

I write as a response to those who have judged me,
put themselves above me,
whilst claiming
To love me.

I write poetry for those who think they don't like it,
I ask them, 'Just try it.'
Close your eyes and let this poem wrap around you...
Do you feel that?

you're inside it.

I write for you,
to make you laugh, to make you cry...
I write for me,
because poetry gives me a natural high as I write it
that I hope to pass on to you as I recite it.

I write for love
I write for lack thereof.

I write for revenge

because I still believe the pen is mightier than the sword
(and I prefer not to fight if I can help it)
and I write when I'm touched by the lives of others,
when I've heard someone's story and I've felt it,
and I wanted to translate it into my words.
Not because I prefer them but because I empathise
and I wanted to retell their story, through my eyes.

I write as a surprise,
for anniversaries, for birthdays...
I write because sometimes I find it hard to express my emotions in
other ways.
I write to share,
I write to become more self-aware.

I write as a tribute to those who inspire me –
not those who know or have known fame –
just those who walk beside me.

I write because I can
I write because that's what I do
I write because that's who I am

I write because...
That's
Who
I
Am.

Muse

Let me out

You know I'm trying to break free
but you just sit there
watching TV
and yet still you wonder why
you're finding it so hard to breathe.

And that sneeze...?
That's not just a cold,
it's this old soul
trying to remind you
of what you already know.

But you keep trying to bury me
like you're *still* not ready.
What is it you're scared of?
Is it really the darkness inside that frightens you, or is it the light?
I'm shining inside you but you keep on insisting the time isn't right.

Or you write about how you can't find the right words.
You've got so many excuses but I think by now I've just about heard
them all.
I watch you as you try to make yourself small
but giants can't hide.
Straighten your back and stop resisting that pride.
You've earned it.

Let me out

I know you can hear me 'cause I'm shouting so loud
trying to make myself heard above the crowd.

You've got so many voices in here telling you you're not good enough.
They're bullies you know, they like to play rough with me
but it's only because they're scared.
You know that, don't you?

They know that when you set me free
they won't be worthy
to share this space in your head,
to take up space in your heart.
They won't be able to keep us apart anymore.

You've let me out before but it's never been for long.
Why is that, did I do something wrong?
I just wanted to show you how much you've achieved.
I just wanted to remind you that it's ok to believe
you're good enough.
Is that too much to ask...?

Let me out

Turn off the internet and open up Word.
Turn off your conscious mind and type, then perhaps I'll be heard
and if that doesn't work..?
We can always get back to basics with a notebook and pen,
see if me and you can reconnect again.

I'd like that.

We're the same,
you and I
I'm in you, yeah
but you're in me too.
I can't work without you.

I know you miss me
when we don't speak for a while.
You go through the motions but I can see that your smile stops
before it reaches your eyes
and although the tears might be a surprise to you,
I see them coming.

And I know that you only really light up
when we're back in touch
'cause I can remind you of who you are
and what life can be about.
So why don't you pick up that pen

And Let. Me. Out.

I carry poems

I carry poems with me,

many different ones each day.
I keep them in my head and heart
and collect more along my way.

My heart is full to bursting
but there'll always be more space
for the poetry I see daily
on almost every face.

I add more poems as I see them
and I see them all the time.
I take mental snapshots of moments,
wrap them in words to make them mine.

I carry the man outside the supermarket with a sleeping bag over his
head.
I carry the words I've still to let go of, those that made me see red.

I carry his frown lines,
I carry her smile,
I carry his laughter,
I carry their sense of style.

I carry the words that lie beneath those that you use.
I carry your pain,
I carry my muse.

I carry all this and more
all of the time,
then give birth to new poems
and hope that you might carry mine.

Still I stand

I stand, unaffected by the sands of time as I wait in line

because I know I'll achieve the future that's rightfully mine in good time.

See, I was born with a pen in my hand and ink runs through my veins

so every emotion can be expressed through rhyme.

My heart is my inkwell, and only when it explodes onto paper do I truly create.

Only when I express myself with truthful reality and allow myself the freedom of thought that I ought to not let escape because it's too... dangerous.

I scare myself with what's hidden deep down inside because that's where I keep the stuff I spent my life trying to hide from.

But maybe that's wrong.

Or maybe I only keep it there because I'm afraid of being psychoanalysed, having mild childhood traumas overdramatised and finding it doesn't even make me feel better.*

Because I run deeper.

I run deeper than tunnel-vision eyes see.

I run deeper than the deepest darkest secrets I only share with those I care for.

I run deeper. And I know there are even more depths to explore if only I can find the right words.

Yes, sometimes I find my creativity stalling but I'll never admit defeat,

I'll just keep on going til I remember those masterpieces I used to write in my sleep while lesser lyricists were still counting sheep.

If you knock me down? I'll just come back fighting, delighting in your surprise to see me still standing when I'd been hearing rumours of my death.

But still I stand.

And I'll continue standing until I finally reach my destination.

Until I land in that place where I'll feel continually de-stressed, a place where I'm constantly conscious I'm God-Blessed.

But for now?

I'll continue to sit with my pen in my hand and let my emotional wounds drop ink drops onto pavement slabs til I leave behind streets stained with these insecurities.

Trauma is trauma, full stop. And I've since had (and still have) therapy, and it did (does) help. If you're considering therapy, please do try it!

PARTS OF
THE POET

*'Every twist and turn in life is an opportunity to
learn something new about yourself.'*
— Jameela Jamil

I used to think I didn't like Jameela Jamil. I mentioned this to my
sister, Lizzie, once, and she was confused. After chatting for a while, so
was I. What was it I 'didn't like' about her? I couldn't put my finger on
it. After all, she seemed to represent everything I believed in. Being
open and honest about her strengths and limitations, having strong
values and living by them, *being willing to change,* and using her
platform for good. 'But', I said to my sister, 'I mean, she's just
everywhere.' I was also annoyed that she seemed to change her mind
about some things over time. Why did this annoy me so much? Isn't
this simply being human? After all, didn't Churchill say, 'If you never
change your mind, you never change anything'? Jameela was (is!)
changing things. And that's a good thing.

It took a while, but I realised my problem with Jameela wasn't with
her at all. It was me. I was angry with myself for not speaking up
about things that were important to me. I was angry with those who

told me, 'You've changed', as I moved through my life journey, leaving me feeling as though it was a bad thing, that we as humans should remain static, stuck at a point in time that perhaps better suited others.

Why am I mentioning all this? Well, this section represents parts of me that have been more or less present at different points in time (and like life, the poems are not ordered in a linear way). Often, the 'darkness' I speak of is, in fact, me folding back inside myself for fear of speaking up, being fully myself (not masking), and being rejected. I'm slowly learning that speaking up (stepping into the 'light' I so often refer to) is a massive part of the healing journey, and, as Jameela demonstrates, by sharing the imperfect path of our ever-developing brains, we give others permission to share their imperfect selves too.

Thanks, Jameela, for shining a mirror on my need for growth, and thanks, Lizzie, for always asking the right questions.

Darkness

Sometimes the darkness frightens me,
I think it might be hiding something.
Other times I like the way
it makes everything
into nothing.

Outside the box

I like it here in my quiet little box.
It's dark, and slightly damp… But it's familiar.

But then you told me that it's alright, that we could go outside,
You said there had never been any need for us to hide.
'Come on out,' you said, 'there's this big ball of light…
They call it "the sun", it's so warm and bright!
Come join me, come feel the glorious sun caress the back of your neck!'

But I didn't believe you, so I told you I wasn't ready yet.
'I'll just stay here for now,' I said, 'in my quiet little box…
Yes it's dark, and slightly damp… But it's familiar.'

Puddles

It rained for a long time,
Just over two years.
Then, gradually, it stopped.

The rain still comes, sometimes.
I'm usually prepared,
I see it coming.

The puddles though,
They appear out of nowhere
And their depth can still take me by surprise.

Sometimes I wish…

Sometimes I wish I could unzip my skin,
clear out all the earthly crap in one go
and have my cleansed spirit step back in…

Just start my life over
without doing 'the work'
but that's not how things work…

'We're here for each other,' my mum used to say
but we're not all for each other, and that's ok.
We all have our own gifts to share
and those who are here to receive them
will eventually appear…

And as for 'the work'?
I promise it's worth it.
Even though sometimes it still makes me want to run,
the secret is to radically accept the bittersweet chaos of an imperfect
life,
and embrace the fact that the work
is never
'done'.

Awkwardly

I don't know what you see
as you look at me
but today I stand here,
awkwardly.

I used to be confident, said I was ready to rise
but later when I looked deeper inside,
it felt wrong,
like it had all been a lie.

I compared myself to those who came before me
and I always came up short.
Up against people who really had something to say
I was simply sharing random thoughts.

Afraid of being exposed
for the fraud I felt myself to be,
I crept into the shadows
where no one could see through me.

I embraced the dark clouds that descended
and with my back to the light,
I clung to them like a security blanket
and kept right out of sight.
I felt that my creativity had deserted me
And that this – the poetry –

just wasn't me
and I discovered that if you believe something,
Then so it will be.

I listened to my demons

and as we walked side by side.
We agreed that I was worthless
and should continue to hide.

But something inside started stirring
as through the dark I saw a sliver of light.
My demons cowered behind me
and I decided the time was right.

Slowly I stood up
and took the offering I now know to be mine.
Right now I hold this light carefully in my hand
but in time, with this, I'll remember, I shine.

I had forgotten that the words were simply an extension of me
but my awakening brings me back here before you,
trying to remember the me I used to be.
Awkwardly.

Onion

I take an onion from the bowl.
The skin comes away in my hand, and
I wrap my fingers around the satisfying crunch
and watch the pieces fall away as I re-open.

I remove the translucent film that remains
and the smell hits me. Earthy, tangy, strong.
This is way stronger than I anticipated
but good, better.

I inhale and my head spins a little.
It's overwhelming.
The knife is sharp and I cut slowly,
savouring the sound of the blade against the chopping board.

Metal on wood. It's reassuring somehow.
As the layers fall away, I fill up.
When I get to the heart, my eyes cloud over.

Salty splashes land silently on the counter.
I'm fine, really. It's just…
This onion
is stronger
than I expected.

Rain

Today, the rain does not soothe me.
Each drop splashes sorrows,
shadows swallowing my soul.

Questions, questions...
A thunderstorm of introspection,
in which I find myself wanting.

Always wanting,
Never enough.

No matter how hard I try
to Rise
clouds still gather
darkening these skies.

I reach into the darkness
seeking just a sliver of light.
Something to cling to
so the storm doesn't consume me
because this time, I feel it just might...

I can take the battering,
each time my skin thickening
but, despite the resilience of my skin,
my soul feels paper thin.
Such a struggle to maintain...

I fear that the rain
may wash away what remains.

Sleepless weeks

It's almost 3am and raised voices invade my dreams.
Heavily whispered threats followed by insults screamed
nudging me gradually wide awake
with rapid pulse rate.

As I wonder if this fight will be fought with weapons of words or
weapons of steel
I listen in silence to see how the mood feels.
It's their arguments these boys should have spent their time
sharpening
I hear the blunt weapons with which they try to tear out each other's
heartstrings.

I move to watch from the window as clumsy lies fly from bored lips
often missing targets but weaker egos seem to take blows in face,
stomach and hips.
The same fight it seems, several times in the past few weeks,
insults thrown round carelessly, emotional wounds staining these
streets.

There's no respite as they fight for hours.
Over time they stop trying to drop their voices and start getting
louder.

Perhaps they have nothing better to do
because they clearly aren't working.
Are they responsibility shirking
or victims of a system that's working against them? I doubt it.
But that's a biased opinion, I've never asked them about it.

A car pulls up and they disperse.
Someone's called the police but these boys are well rehearsed

so they just stand on corners talking in hushed tones with their friends
until the police car turns round the bend,
then the verbal punches continue and suggested violence ensues.
They talk of the need to show respect, whilst hurling abuse.

At this point I know no injuries beyond wounded pride will be
sustained
so I lie back in bed but even as their voices die down they still remain
under my window fighting just loud enough to keep me awake
and when my alarm sounds at 6,
my eyes still ache.

Words

I love, and yet fear, the power of words
because they remain on in my heart long after they've been heard.
I have been healed with words some have spoken
and yet with those same words, I can also
be broken.

A comment made some time ago, probably without thinking
can come to mind and even now, I still feel my heart sinking.

The same words each time cut just as deep.
Although I think they've been forgotten,
they return to steal my sleep.

A promise of love he had no intention of keeping,
a beautiful lie, whispered while he thought I was sleeping.
A friend who believed my soul was impure,
her words twice as sharp
because her heart was so sure.

But then words can also keep loved ones close despite the distance
between us
or even make my day, though at the time seeming meaningless.
The words that accompany affection maternal
confirming a love I know to be eternal
or a compliment from a stranger I just happen to pass,
my 'thanks' lost in the wind
But in my smile, it lasts.

And then...

Sometimes the words we speak loudest are the ones we don't say
like the declaration of love that should have been made yesterday

or the truth, that should have been told at the start
before it came out too late, and shattered a heart.

I love, and yet fear, the power of words.
They remain on in my heart long after they've been heard.
I have been healed with words some have spoken
and yet with those same words, I can also
be broken.

And so I leave you, hoping I've used the right words –
those that remain with you, after they've been heard.

Needle and thread

Yellow, red, golden thread.
A button rainbow and cowrie shells.
Sunlight pouring in through an open window
reminds me of holidays and revitalised, I fall
into the soft embrace of creation
and, fuelled by mango juice, I write.

My hunger sated,
the energy these women have created
fills me up.
The mirror reflects
Beauty, Strength, Love.
I am relaxed
I am refreshed
I am awake
I am.

White noise

For you, it's a comforting silence,
the sort that puts babies to sleep.
For me, it takes on human form,
grows nails that dig in deep.

For you,
it's the gentle hum of a washing machine.
For me, it's a whispered threat,
a strangled, low-pitched scream.

You hear fuzzy static,
I feel a semi-automatic
and see white spots before my eyes
and as you sigh contentedly,
I climb inside myself and cry.

You hear these sounds as silence,
they signal the end of the day.
I feel them and they're measured violence,
looking for words to slay.

You focus on this white noise
and can lose yourself in flow.
I feel like my thoughts drown in it,
the words don't know where to go.

So they hide somewhere safe, somewhere deep in my chest
where I might keep those memories I feel are better left repressed.
Then when I struggle to bring them back
I label this internal fight, and call myself depressed.

But today I realised I had a mute button all along,

I can turn off all the white noise and replace it with a song.
Step back into my silence,
and release the words as they grow strong.

Then, as they travel through me
without the need to fight,
they lose the heavy stickiness
and start to feel soft and light.

Then, as they gently land
I wonder how I can
show you how much they give me
with their firm, yet gentle, touch.

Silent scream*

A silent scream comes from within. It pierces through the noise of the external world like a bullet plunges into the soft flesh of a living body. No-one hears. But the pain is like waiting for tomorrow to come.
It grips the throat and squeezes until the inside is outside and the outside is no longer a reality but a dream from the depths of the imagination and life...
Ceases to exist.

I wrote this poem during an A-Level exam in 1995! I was getting stuck and couldn't focus, so to shift my attention, I started freewriting. This was the result! If you're wondering, I did go on to finish the exam, and pass! This is what I mean when I say sometimes I write in the way many people doodle. I was releasing something around not being 'enough' to show up in full. Something I'm constantly working on and love helping others with!

Would you, could you

Would you wrap me up in a wish you didn't realise you held
This close?

Could you let your dreams roam free,
Walk hand in hand with forgotten ghosts?

Would you break down barriers to get to the other side?

Or would you revert to type,
Lay down inside yourself
And hide.

Could you let yourself see what you already know, and
Without looking down, could you learn to…

Let Go.

This jigsaw

This jigsaw
lies in pieces
on the floor.

Some of the pieces look the same
but I know they're not.
Not really.

If I put them back in the wrong place
the picture will be completely different
to the one on the front of the box.

But maybe that's ok.
Maybe the picture I end up with
doesn't have to be the one that was suggested.

Perhaps the box didn't know
how much more
these pieces could be.

The perfect moment

As I lie here on the greenest grass, still warm from the afternoon sun,
I find myself looking up into the clearest, bluest sky.
Without intention, I empty my mind
and that's when I feel her presence beside me.

She slips her hand in mine
and tells me her name.
'But don't say it aloud,' she whispers,
'If you look too hard for me, you may not find me again.'
So we lie there hand in hand, Happiness and I
in companionable silence, just watching the cloudless sky.

PEOPLE-WATCHING

I used to play a game when I was younger. It involved turning off the sound on the TV and imagining what the characters were saying. I guess it was a kind of improv – perhaps I got the idea from drama class? I don't remember. But it's a lot like people-watching.

We don't know what's going on in other people's lives. This is true whether it's someone we interact casually with every day, like the same cashier in the supermarket because you always go in at the same time, a colleague you exchange pleasantries with but never really *talk* to, other parents in the school playground or simply those you see passing by as you sit in a cafe or on a park bench idly observing your surroundings. We make up stories about other people all the time – this is where unconscious bias comes from (and we are all guilty of this, at some level). It's just human nature. We observe life through the filter of our own experiences and, in some cases, project those experiences onto what we observe. This is where judgement, or being judgemental of others (and of ourselves!), comes from.

It's also where empathy comes from. By watching others *without* judgement, we can get curious about them. What might they be struggling with? What might they have to offer the world? Do they know that just by existing, they may be inspiring those around them in ways they can't even begin to imagine?

Some of these poems are about strangers I've quietly observed but will never meet, some are about people I know, or have known. You may even find yourself (or a version of yourself) here.

'The quieter you become, the more you are able to hear.'

– Rumi

People-watching

Man on the bench with a big smile on your face,
tell me your secret… What makes you so high?
Woman on the train, holding your paper up high to hide the tears in
your eyes…
Why do you hurt so much, what made you cry?

This child at the bus stop with an infectious giggle,
your good humour is contagious and I laugh out loud myself.
I try to carry your outlook around with me all day,
a reminder of the true meaning of wealth.

The old couple sharing a picnic in the park
needing nothing more than the fact they are still together…
The young couple sitting down there by the river
lost in love, promising each other forever.

Two friends in a restaurant catching up on old times,
eyes lit up as you reminisce.
A child blowing out the candles on a birthday cake,
eyes tightly shut with your secret wish.

Old man in a pub talking to friends,
telling elaborate stories of days gone by.
Teenage boy with your head in your hands,
telling yourself that real men don't cry (they should).

These are the scenes I see as I walk the streets,
scenes I couldn't ignore if I tried.
Snapshots of the lives of people I'll never meet,
who see me as nothing more
than a casual passerby.

Berets, and all that jazz

At lunchtime
we talked of jazz clubs
and those pretentious intellectuals
finger clicking in a haze of smoke.

Wearing berets and
attaching unnecessary meaning to music
that needs no explanation
because, we all agreed,
the music simply speaks for itself.

I saw a girl on the tube that night
wearing a purple beret.
I heard finger clicks in my ears
and wondered whether she thought
my notebook was pretentious.

Small talk*

'Morning.'
We both throw words on the table.
Seemingly meaningless,
reheating recent connection.

An almost-formed thought
dances between us.
I catch the abstract,
try to reframe it.
He nods and in our own way
we both reclaim it.

'Morning.'
Her eyes don't match her tone,
not yet.
Warm words are offered and she accepts.
This gentle heat will make her stronger
once we've heard and held her.

'I'm glad.'
Sharing photos
her smile lights her eyes.
She shares more small parts,
revealing some of her soul
and we strengthen the collective whole.

'Hey.'
Her words bounce between us
gently poking the stronger bonds,
giving permission to be more playful.
A reminder that I'm grateful...

This small talk
is bigger than it looks.

For all my colleagues, old and new, at Wholegrain Digital. For always making the space for something bigger than small talk.

Small change

You don't like the weight of it
in your pocket
so when you get home
you transfer it to a suitable wallet.

Then you only retrieve the coins
you feel worthy of your attention.
The copper ones, you tell me,
don't deserve retention.

So you step out
carrying only silver and gold,
for these are the colours of grown-up currency.
This is the belief you've been sold.

And you've bought it and you've taught it
and it has become universally true.
So that even when I show you the value can be the same,
you'll argue until you're blue.

Then as the colour rises (I see it on your face),
you say that in your pocket
(and therefore the world)
these coins don't have a place.

You keep saying that they're worthless
and as they start to believe this is true,
they start disappearing
until they're almost invisible to you.

One day I'll bag them up
and take them to the bank,

I'll get them changed into gold coins and notes
and some might say you ought to thank me.

But that's not why I'll do this.
I'll do it because I hope you'll then return the belief you've been sold
and see this small change as something more, not worthless...
You'll see that it's worth its weight
in Gold.

Celebrity

Perhaps she wears sunglasses
so as not to be blinded by her own light.
I wonder why
she's still fighting it.

Melting pot*

A burst of foreign flavours explodes on London's tongue.
It's so intense she has to stop and catch her breath,
re-fill her smoke-filled lungs.

She speaks in tongues,
300+ voices, all with something different to say...
Each individual ingredient making this city the dish that you and I
taste today.

She inhales the heady aroma of at least 14 different faiths
practised by over 40 communities of different races
of which over 10,000 people were born outside of the UK.

She stirs in a pinch of each country's history
and as she does, she unveils some of the mysteries
that contributed to an old fear of the unknown.

She gives us a taste that shows us that with each extra dash of spice,
with each slice of these different lives...
We can make a dish that nourishes both our hearts, and our minds.
She chooses the fabric for her wedding sari and has henna painted on
her hands.

On the bank holiday weekend she strolls along Brighton beach hand
in hand with her man,
eating fish and chips, her naked feet sinking into the sand.

At carnival the steel drums play out a rhythm her heart always knew
and she doesn't even have to think because her feet already seem to
know exactly what to do.

A Serbian folk song dances through her head.

She hits the snooze button on her alarm cause she's not yet ready to
get out of bed.
She says a prayer of thanks that she's lived to see another day;
that she was granted asylum.

She wipes away a tear for those she lost to the war and tells herself
that in the next life,
she'll see them again
but right now? She's just happy that she's safe.

She dips her spoon into this mix, brings it to her lips
and takes a sip.
She adds a little more seasoning to this melting pot
and before she eats,

she gives thanks for what she's got.

*A version of this poem was originally written in 2005 as a commission for a
Diversity in the Community event.*

A quiet presence

It's been a long time
since I last saw him.
I think maybe
I'd missed him, a bit.
Certainly that quiet presence.*
You can almost hear the words
before he voices them.

His hair's a bit longer
but he still looks the same,
I think.
He has 'lovable soul'
written all over his face,
which hasn't aged.
He looks happy.

*This 'quiet presence' is Niall O'Sullivan. I wrote this poem during an open mic night
at the Poetry cafe in the mid-2000s. Thanks for the inspiration, Niall!

Mercury

She moves like mercury.
Touches everything but leaves no trace.
Shining from within,
her light projecting onto others' faces.
Giving them something to fill that empty   space   with.

Rush hour

A mustard wax jacket with
corduroy collar and cuffs.
Flame red hair.
Her primary palette an exclamation mark
among the muted suits.

Glitter

Stratford Circus cafe:

Glitter, gold and green,
on Brown skin.
Smilingly shyly, she apologises
for her appearance.
She is in a play, she explains.

Later, on the bus:

Gold and green,
on Brown skin.
Lips defiantly orange.
Hair piled perfectly high.
A loose strand tucked neatly away
with manicured hands.
She does not apologise
for herself.

MY
MOTIVATION

'It's like a thread, connecting me to all those I love...
But some are different. They're more like... umbilical
cords... my son, obviously. But also those I love in
that family way. These cords have an ethereal glow
about them. They're hard to break, as they should be.'

I said this in a therapy session some time ago when discussing
unhealthy attachments and healthy ones and what the difference felt
like (and this visual was how I could best explain it). The ones with
the ethereal umbilical cord attachments are the people I consider
family.

Some are by blood, but family is not only (and not always) defined by
blood ties. This section is dedicated to these people; they are the ones
who inspire and motivate me daily, whether they are here with me in
body or now in spirit.

I hope these poems give you pause to think about the journeys you have been on with your most nourishing relationships, whether by birth or by choice, and what that connection means to you.

More than the earth (Mum)

You gave me the most selfless gift of all...
You supported me in Success,
you'd pick me up when I fall.
There for me always I know I could depend.
More than a Mother, you became my friend.

You are the love to which I always return
because home is where the heart is, this much I have learned.
You gave us all love and helped us to grow
by teaching us our worth,
and then letting go.

So no one could judge you by anything other than this:
The affections of your children,
the truth behind a kiss.
For only those you raised to adulthood know your true worth:
More than all the stars in the heavens,
More than the earth.

Lizzie

Curled up inside yourself,
still I used to think you so bold.
It's truly been a privilege
to see more and more of you unfold.

Defined by our experiences,
we've had our fair share of downs.
But hold on, we're not nearly done...
More ups will come around.

Consistently sisterly
since the day you were born.
We offer each other shelter
to weather life's many storms

And in all of the spaces
between the rain,
phoenix-like, we rise.
And you (will always)
light life's stage again.

Lawrence

At home
you are the only one who will tolerate me singing,
it puts you to sleep.
Later you tell me
that was just to shut me up.

In the park, you are my responsibility
but I turn my back for a minute and you fall.
I see it in slow motion.
You cry and blood spatters from your mouth
but you're ok, you're tougher than you look.

From a baby bow tie and
mini Michael Jackson impersonations
to 'Eat my shorts,' ad infinitum, as
reruns of the Simpsons
play on a loop in the background.

From a payphone in corridors with ears
I call home and don't recognise your voice.
You're no longer a child, but I didn't notice you changing.

You think I'm cool.
That doesn't last.

From Afro,
to cornrows,
to cut low...

From choir boy,
to b-boy,
from boy... to man.

Life ages us both.
You now have life experience beyond your years
and I value your advice.
I wish that I was as laid-back
as you appear to be.

Playing mermaids

It's a sunny Saturday afternoon
as we walk up to the school's open-air pool,
talking about the boy who smiles with his eyes
and how we hate that people still buy us the same outfit in different sizes
even though there's four years between us.

We get changed quickly because the changing room smells of feet and sweat
and the sticky heat makes my hair cling to the back of my neck.
The pool's busy with harassed parents trying to control over-excited
kids who've never had this much fun at school
and teenage girls eyeing up the lifeguards who are too busy posing to
notice because they think it makes them look cool.

We dive into the water and at first the chlorine stings my eyes
but I soon acclimatise.
We swim around underwater until we have to surface to breathe
but the sounds around the pool assault my ears
and I immediately go back under, where I feel so much more at ease.

We play mermaids for hours
until the wrinkly skin on our fingers and toes
reminds us it's almost time to go.
But still, we stay under til we feel the pressure on our lungs
and start to taste the hunger forming on our tongues.

Deliciously tangy pickled onion crisps are the best thing I've eaten all week
washed down with raspberry panda pops,
the syrupy drink fizzing like liquid bubblegum as I hold it in my cheeks.

Rubbery pink foam shrimps leave their sugary smell on our fingers
and thumbs,
one of many smells that can still take me back to that mermaid
summer.

Heading home, exhausted but content,
we walk in companionable silence
and consider it a day well spent.
Whenever I inhale that same delicious scent of summer dusk,
it reminds me that from that day to this, nothing can come between us.

Sam

University Halls.
Bars and clubs.
Blue cocktails, crop tops, short skirts
(they now call that 'Y2K aesthetic').
You make me laugh.
We drift apart.

September 11th, Baker Street.
We reconnect with
underground hip-hop nights, and
de-briefs in the park.

When I am broken
you pick up the pieces,
remind me of my worth.
I hope I do
the same for you.

We run around eating pineapples,
drinking champagne cocktails
and long island iced teas.
Laughing.

September 26th, Liverpool Street.
My world comes tumbling down.
You fly to my side
with pumpkin seeds, crisps and hugs.

You hold me up when my feet fail me.

I have no doubt
that we'll always walk side by side,
you and I.
And that laughter will be the backbeat of our lives.

Spring rolls at the Science Museum

We sit
side by side on a bench
at the Science Museum,
eating spring rolls.

I recall Chinese takeaways and
picking the prawns out of my special fried rice.
You comment that this will be a new memory, in time.
I hadn't thought of that.

The next time
l have a spring roll
I wonder whether I'll recall
childhood memories or
sitting next to you
at the Science Museum,
talking about remembering now.

This is The Work

For the 100th time
she scans her work,
checking she's adequately represented
these voices, too seldom heard.

Accessible format, black text on white.
The results of years of working before dawn and late into the night,
checking she has all her citations right.
Wondering, as she recalls her own words,
whether quoting herself is slightly absurd.

She finishes and no one claps,
something of an anticlimax
after pouring her soul into this work for more than 10 years,
her understanding of grief now transcends polite tears.

As she prepares to hit submit
she reclaims the proper spelling of her own name and that's when it
hits...
Just how much of her identity is tied up in this.

She wonders whether this thesis is enough
to contain all the 'stuff'.
A poor word for the experiences she's witnessed
that necessitate rage
against a system that denies humanity with seemingly innocent words
on a page.

No papers.

This is her work.
After a decade it still feels like we've only just begun

to make a difference.

But she can't stop now.

This is her.
This is the work that needs to be done.
This is The Work.

Shine

If I shine, that's your reflection.
I'm simply mirroring back aspects of your own perfection.
I try to reflect the best of those I keep around me.
And when ravens circle overhead,
I remember the light that surrounds me.

Darkness regularly tries to pull me down,
but you named me a Queen, and I try to retain that crown.
When I lose my voice and concern myself with how much I haven't
done,
you remind me of just how far I've come.

Your light guides me back to the right path, my strength renewed,
I can't help but reflect it back on you.
So when you think it's my wings that have helped you climb this high,
remember it was you, who taught me, how to fly.

THE FUTURE

I'll keep it simple. This section is about, and dedicated to, my son.

It was author Elizabeth Stone who said, 'Making the decision to have a child – it is momentous. It is to decide forever to have your heart go walking around outside your body.' I thought I understood that quote the first time I heard it, but I didn't, not really. Not until I had my son.

I still continue to understand it more and more as we move through the different seasons of life together (as I write this, he is at the tween/teen stage, and I am post-menopausal. It's an interesting season!). My son has been – and continues to be – my greatest teacher.

Whether by default or design, Oberon, I learn something new from you every day, and, as I am always reminding you,

There is nothing you can do that will make me stop loving you. Nothing.

Sky

At the park
You look up in wonder.

'Sky,' I say, pointing

You smile and reach out
As if to touch it.

I hope you never stop trying.

God is a P

'I don't think God is an old white man
with a beard, sitting on a cloud,'
my son says, looking to me for a response.
'Well, neither do I...' I begin.

He looks off into the distance.
'I think God', he says,
'is a Black man. And He definitely doesn't have a beard.'
'So you do think God is a He?'
He turns slowly, to look at me.

'No Mummy, I'm just saying that
God probably wears shorts
and looks like you or me.
He could even be that man on the street

But... God can be any person.
Boy, Girl, or... I don't know.
God is not a He or a She...
God, I think... Is a P.'

The lighthouse

He tells me the lighthouse looks small.
'Not at all,'
I reply. 'What makes you think it needs to be big?'
He refers me to Peppa Pig.
'Ah yes, that one is tall.
But it doesn't need to be, not at all.'
I tell him that what's important about the lighthouse
is one thing, and one alone –
that the light inside shines bright enough
to guide those lost at sea,
so they can find their way back home.

Safe space

'Click the door shut'
he always says.
I think it makes him feel safe,
enclosing his space.

That summer,
he stood on stage and spoke out loud,
showed me where he feels proud.

Just now,
he left the door open.
I didn't say anything.

Fix you

I cannot even begin to hold the concept
of how much love I have for you.

I promise
I will fight for you
with every breath,
with whatever I have left

and I will never
EVER
try

to 'fix' you.*

*This was written during a period when my son was obsessed with Coldplay's 'Fix
You ', specifically, a YouTube video of acapella group Naturally 7 covering this song.
He would watch it repeatedly and then listen until he fell asleep. This was also during
a period when it was becoming even more clear that he showed up differently in the
world (although it took another six years for an appropriate diagnosis), and many
believed he was intentionally challenging and thus, needed to be 'fixed'. This song still
brings up strong feelings for me every time I hear it.

MEDITATIONS

'This sauce will thicken on standing.'

This section is simply five short meditations, including the title poem.

All were written during moments of mindfulness or deep reflection. Most are short enough to be read while breathing deeply – perhaps one deep breath in, and a long breath out as you absorb these words, and then on with your day.

I hope they offer you a moment of peace.

Breathe

Breathe in.
Close your eyes.
Hold on.

1, 2, 3, 4, 5.

And now…
Breathe out, with an audible sigh.
Drop your shoulders
but keep your head, high.

And repeat.
Repeat.
Repeat.

Boiling

Tiny bubbles, silent at first,
grow to noisy bursts of soft sound.
Time stands still.
I almost forget to add the pasta.

Nostalgia

A pillow of sugary pink confection
licked by flickering orange tongues
blisters black,
cracks.
Sticky pink lava melts,
taking me back.

Swim

Hot sun.
Warm skin.
Cool water.
Dive in.
Swim.

Sauce will thicken on standing

Blend ingredients.
Boil.
Turn down the heat.
Leave it alone
(I mean it).

Don't interfere with the process.
Just trust
this sauce
will thicken
on standing.

THANK YOU

Before a more traditional acknowledgements page, I wanted to thank all those who made this book happen — whether you told me to go for it or believed I couldn't, or wouldn't, do it, you're all part of my journey, so thank you. The words below are for those of you who help me keep the shadows behind me.

I'd been walking hand in hand with demons and kissing the dark,
hiding in the shadows behind the heart...
But then angels brushed my face with their wings as through the
silence I hear you sing
and I know I am blessed.

Some of you know me so much better than you think,
you swim out to hold me just as I'm about to sink.
Some of you show me a new perspective,

show me the danger of being too introspective.

Some of you shine so bright the light hurts my eyes.
Always behind me, you teach me to fly.
To the one who was always there – before I was projecting.

You were born with wings of your own; you don't need protecting.
Some of you think that you don't do so much for me.
You don't know how much what you do touches me.
Some of you teach me what I already know.
All of you mean more to me than these words can show.

You are the stars that light up my sky,
you are the angels that walk by my side.
Because when I feel I'm alone in the dark
I see the light that shines from your hearts
and I know I am blessed.

Thank you for being my angels, my stars.
Thank you for being those who light up my dark.

ACKNOWLEDGMENTS

First and foremost, I have to thank my son, Oberon, for asking the 'what's stopping you?' question I most ask of others, in his own way, when he said (many times), 'If you're a poet, you should have a book. Why don't you?' My reasons were not real reasons, more excuses. So here we are. Thank you, son. x

On a more practical note, I'd like to thank all those who have encouraged and directly helped me to improve my writing in many ways. Mr Letters, who taught me to see that my poetry could have purpose (whether he liked it or not!), Amy Beeson and Sarah Beeson MBE, The What I'm Writing group (especially Maddy, Renée and Sophie). Teika, for giving me feedback on the initial draft of this collection when I first thought I *might* publish it! I'd also like to thank all those who were part of my spoken word journey – Agnes Meadows, John-Paul O'Neill, Niall O'Sullivan, Kat Francois, 'Other' Theresa, Beyonder, Inua Ellams, Musa Okwonga, Joshua Idehen, Naomi Woddis, Ebele and more I'm forgetting to mention (sorry!).

Thanks to Helen Drake and Ali Plowright. You know what for.

Of course, massive thanks to Nicola and the team at the Unbound Press for bringing this book to life! Thanks for first meeting me in the dreamscape first, Nicola, and planting the seed, and thanks for holding the space (leaving the sauce to thicken!) for this, and future projects, to arrive as and when they're supposed to.

Thanks to my super soul sisters Lizzie and Sam. Lizzie, for choosing to share this earthly journey with me – and for always asking the right questions! Sam - for repeatedly showing me that we don't need to be anything or anyone but ourselves – that we are always enough, just as we are. Thanks also to Lawrence and Sarah for your never-ending support.

My Sri Lanka sister group – Thanks for being a safe space for reflective growth and shared celebration.

Yesim – thanks for the feedback, for being an excellent additional co-parent/platonic life partner and providing unending, ever-thoughtful personal – and invaluable professional – support. We are definitely from the same soup!

Charlie & Mike – I cannot think of one of you without the other. Thanks for arriving with hair still wet from the bath (Charlie) when you ever think I might need you, and for helping me armour up for battle (Mike) when I'm about to give up on myself.

Danny – for always believing in me. I wish I'd told you more how much I believed in you.

Thanks, Tom & Vineeta and the entire Wholegrain Digital team, for making work feel like home, whether I am there in person or spirit. Thanks for seven+ years of support, kid (not baby!) sitting, cat sitting and cold swimming!

Last, but certainly not least, thanks to Mum, for always believing in me, even (especially) when I didn't believe in myself.

ABOUT THE AUTHOR

Rachael B is a freelance writer, poet and personal coach. She refers to herself as a 'self-care activist and growth catalyst,' to describe the work she does to facilitate personal and professional growth, offering a gentle, non-judgemental space for both.

When it comes to writing, poetry is her first love. The words that flow through her help to make sense of her experiences, acting as a catalyst for personal growth. She hopes they may do the same for those who feel drawn to read them.

She's currently working on her second collection, which will use poetry as therapy to empower women who have experienced emotional and/or physical abuse to re-write their stories.

Website: www.reallyrachaelb.com
Instagram: @ReallyRachaelB
LinkedIn: linkedin.com/in/rachaelb2021/